HOME IN

poems by
JORIS SOEDING

Home in Nine Moons $12.00
Poems by Joris Soeding
Clare Songbirds Publishing House Poetry Series
ISBN 978-1-947653-30-6
Clare Songbirds Publishing House
Home in Nine Moons © 2018 Joris Soeding
All Rights Reserved. Clare Songbirds Publishing House retains right to reprint.
Permission to reprint individual poems must be obtained from the author who owns the copyright.
cover design © 2018 Clare Songbirds Publishing House

Printed in the United States of America
FIRST EDITION

Clare Songbirds Publishing House Mission Statement:
Clare Songbirds Publishing House was established to provide a print forum for the creation of limited edition, fine art from poets and writers, both established and emerging. We strive to reignite and continue a tradition of quality, accessible literary arts to the national and international community of writers, and readers. Chapbook manuscripts are carefully chosen for their ability to propel the expansion of art and ideas in literary form. We provide an accessible way to promote the art of words in order to resonate with, and impact, readers not yet familiar with the siren song of poets and writers. Clare Songbirds Publishing House espouses a singular cultural development where poetry creates community and becomes commonplace in public places.

140 Cottage Street
Auburn, New York 13021
www.ClareSongbirdspub.com

Contents

I.

At the Free Clinic	11
The Last Swarm	12
Unsmudged	13
The Body Away	14
Four States Away	15
Framing the Moon	16
As Birth	17
Counting and the Blue Envelope	18
Departing Shower	19
October as Mute	20
Four a.m. Soliloquy	21
Two	22
Sold	23
Christmas, Siesta Key	24

II.

The Pope and Rendition without a Count	26
On Seeing *30 Days of Night*, By Myself	27
Ode to Yvette Vickers	28
Proposing to Miss Make-Believe	29
Red Hands near Six Lanes	30
After the Funeral, Hamburg	31
ER, Friday Night	32
At Mr. Weiner's	33
On Seeing *I, Robot*, By Myself	34
When Tucson Came for Amanda	35

III.

Painting at First Light	40
The Southbound Untitled	41
A Peninsula as Lover Then Son	42
To Downtown in July	43
Starved in the Accidental	44
Six Bags of Barbie	45

Descent into Denver	46
To Downtown in October	47
White Mist at Bunker Hill	48
Vater, Ich Schlafe Nicht or Father, I Am Not Sleeping	49
Dusk and the Daughter Named Isabel	50

IV.

Dealey Plaza	52
On Seeing *The Revenant*, By Myself	53
To Bryce or Victoria	54
April in Harbor Springs	55
A Day with My Daughter	56
Summer Drive	57
Home in Nine Moons	58
Black Friday	61

Thank you for home: Christa, Blake, Victoria, Mami and Papa, the Poskozim family.

I have a lot of gratitude for the supportive teachers I had in which several of these poems were first drafted and shared in their classes.

I am very appreciative for the wonderful blurbs I have received from authors for this collection and my chapbooks.

Grateful acknowledgement is made to the editors of the following publications in which these poems previously appeared:

Apocalypse: "Six Bags of Barbie"

Briller Magazine: "After the Funeral, Hamburg," "At Mr. Weiner's," "Dusk and the Daughter Named Isabel," "Four States Away," "Painting at First Light," "Summer Drive," "To Bryce or Victoria," "To Downtown in July"

Chicago Literati: "Four a.m. Soliloquy," "Red Hands near Six Lanes"

City Works: "A Peninsula as Lover Then Son," "The Southbound Untitled"

Columbia Chronicle: "The Body Away," "Departing Shower," "Unsmudged"

Columbia Poetry Review: "The Last Swarm"

Concho River Review: "At the Free Clinic"

Courier: "Four a.m. Soliloquy"

HEART: "At the Free Clinic," "ER, Friday Night"

Hobo Camp Review: "As Birth," "Counting and the Blue Envelope," "Home in Nine Moons"

Into the Teeth of the Wind: "Ode to Yvette Vickers"

MiPOesias: "On Seeing *I, Robot*, By Myself"

Pebble Lake Review: "The Pope and Rendition without a Count," "Proposing to Miss Make-Believe"

The Prose-Poem Project: "Framing the Moon"

Red River Review: "Sold"

San Pedro River Review: "Starved in the Accidental," "Vater, Ich Schlafe Nicht or Father, I Am Not Sleeping"

SEEDS: "When Tucson Came for Amanda"

Spillway: "On Seeing *30 Days of Night*, By Myself"

for Mami and Papa

I.

At the Free Clinic

not a cloud in Uptown this Monday
they seem to all be in the waiting room

even the car is parked on Sunnyside Avenue
behind a plate from Kansas

someone argues with the secretary,
whose response is, "save it"
I wait properly behind the yellow line

the brick wall something out of movies
just one little push
same should be for a second TB shot
though without a memento of luck

a man attempts to nap
leaning into the bookshelf

the only child here stares at me

heads tilted for each mispronounced name

if only Keats had this
these vaccinations

spilt coffee with cream a shade lighter than the staircase

outside they seek more with shopping carts
a styrofoam cup is flicking across the pathetic grass
the mural on an end of a thrift store reads,
"…and God said it was good."

The Last Swarm

I scratch the plagues
smear the rain
so one moon once mine
cuts dim and green ends

if her pills find ten arms
bend the blue shade
hum three words
and touch the blind

I was more ice than June
they said
lost the burned storm
so sand was frail

I taste the cold name
ash once skin
I sleep and play
like red glass dolls

Unsmudged

I had reached the age of needing
to bend my legs in the bathtub
looking down those thighs
icebergs in a warm ocean
water in perfect stillness
until hands made the breaking
to announce make-believe creatures underneath
spilling across islands of that skin
I became waves of nighttime seas
these were the quiet moments as a boy

The Body Away

I am beginning to form

        a man's
        face

not even
      the yesterday
                        or child of I

has this morning's resemblance

                    the near unnoticed
                    of gentle mutations

hair blending
        into sides
                of hands
                      like a slow plague

I am
welded
            into the hummed orchestra of my fathers

Four States Away

four boys on the court, white shirts untucked
tzetses wavering with each jump shot
one of them with a yarmulke in his mouth because of the wind
the tallest puts an arm on his while dribbling

light charcoal in the southward sky
I'd rather practice my free throw or lay-up
than wait for the bus
make a third pot of coffee for the day
and do more work

a cop pulls over a white station wagon
next to the sign that reads, "BLIND"

they are everywhere
since the shooting
not far from where I got a picture in a guillotine at nine
went swimming at Econo Lodge
and always ordered Sprite at restaurants

two other boys stand next to the police car, listening
the conversation quick
the bus arrives

Framing the Moon

It is clear the ball was larger when I was a boy. Not comfy to play with, or close enough, but a ball nevertheless. The undim glow unmatched concrete, sloping downward till it circled. A silver poking through frayed pines (peering through oak trees always blocked the light too much). In front of a silhouette night was the greatest version of grey. I wanted to photograph the ball like postcards at the gift shop of Cape Canaveral, a close-up of earth, the tripod somehow even in between the ball's craters. I didn't even try for the camera. A close-up wouldn't be close at all. The flash would go off. I would have to fly near stars, set up lights on a spaceship with clean windows. I would hope for the best picture of what the ball is for a child.

As Birth
~for Amanda

I am fearing intersections for you
this fragile place of your one bed
a long window in the shared room
so I have arrived
with flowers not for graves
yet returned of absent you
in visitations among the half dead
under sheets

you recite the year
the belt in your perfect teeth
prickling those arms (still red)
I have brushed prior
with implications of night
as recently you nodded, faltered
dropping needles into the sea
on recognizable toilets for balance

whisperings of our summer quietly conquered
stripped to the deaf shrillness of stars
we shall bathe once more
in voices not bodies
where streams lie coiled, strange, untouched
I am still in your forty-four days
this warmed light blue bedside
mountains we have hushed before
tomorrow will not hurt you
I promise

Counting and the Blue Envelope

I have crawled the month to this night. October 28th. Reddishness in the rendezvous. Or maybe no color to retell. Leaves, sidewalk, hair, traffic, our German tongues. Then dark. The dance. And now. And now.

A presidential campaign—in a state never resided more than hours. Movie previews in solitaire. You are presently the stranger. We saw *Seven* in a theatre that no longer exists. Said first I love yous on a park bench that is gone. So we danced and as of late I dreamt your welcoming into the dead. Washing your face, rolled up jeans near the waterfall. Someone closer to ends.

Ten years and not having drowned. Either one of us. Tonight almost ridiculous. Bare. Appropriate moon as always.

The letter you wrote. Princess Diana and Mother Theresa passed. Missing the states. "I'll see you in October."

Departing Shower

perhaps someone
in this bathroom
mirror
without reflection
door
without entrance

October as Mute

it was this intentional violet sky
that I once knew
at six in the morning
with the border of moon
and its last milk
waiting at the bottom

we would be on near-dead water
skimming across Orchard Lake
with perfect cuts of our oars
nine red jackets in approached fog
stillness interrupted
no one could touch
the innocent things we carved

Four a.m. Soliloquy

I'm dreaming dear toads tender swamps
                    until skillful of this bed

you're the snakes in sidewalks
                    leaving patterns for storms to forget

this beauty hints at nervous
                    too close at truly recalling

an act of three flowers
                    dangled from nighttime lampposts

I'm in question marks unlike sleeping
                    glass under a tipsy moon

the chattering of hands
                    have me slipped into corners

Two
~for Mami

a morning of leaves
overwhelmed with appropriate rain

I approach her willing arms
warm lap consistently awry

after breakfast and us being similar
my feet far from the kitchen floor

at the round oak table I cite forever
she hesitates, then tells me that all of us leave sometime

"what if I eat more vegetables?" I ask, in tears
"that will help you live longer," she replies

I glance at the evaporated milk
the label reveals a cow inside a can, head out and grinning

disgusted but able to fork more peas, red cabbage
refer to He-Man as my ideal health goal

I quickly leave the thought of my family gone
being solitary with so many images of heaven and navigation
at six

again peering at rain, trees on a slope
eventually to the table with my mom

Sold

after seventeen months I am frizzling
these rooms of tying my first shoelace
riding the blue bike with a shove from Papa on this stranger-
less street
where I pretended to be He-Man
announcing to each neighbor in a sleeveless undershirt and
plastic, silver sword
more than once a Native-American on Halloween
wanting to be part of a tribe for a long time
hours in the tree house, practicing basketball, swimming
with G.I. Joes and Mami
whiffle ball with Tim next door, the roof being a homerun
at the table outside with Omi and Oma summer after sum-
mer
twenty-five years
too difficult to turn these rooms over
close the door, leave this home, the woods, street, quietly
and quickly

Christmas, Siesta Key

"da sind keine mehr Leute," you say
the world could dissolve tonight with my father
few light spots above the gulf, those insects,
sailboats remain
on our way back from the drum circle
dances in the absence of fire, petals
tide approaches

II.

The Pope and Rendition Without a Count

approaching Seymour and Dunsmuir
you tell me that he's passed
and I was so afraid this morning

even then as boy for the sake of age
wept on Mami's lap, his leaving Detroit on remoteless TV
at dusk waving to the helicopters
just us goodbye, this street and driveway once had

lulled on this sidewalk
indecisive at listing Our Father after Our Father
I feel ashamed
April you are so wicked

inside, away from tonight, ripping ham and pineapple pizza
heroin in much of those hands to alley,
swallow to a wall with filth dried
afterwards Whitman in my bag
slowly it begins to rain
slowly this must all be false

On Seeing *30 Days of Night*, By Myself

the projectionist booth is empty
with the loud muffle at reel's end
then white, a strand of pink
prolonged by dust and few others gathering coats

after standing at the lowest urinal
to not crowd the other two gentlemen
I try to wash the dried blood from my left hand
half a dozen of us
the door closes
alone without glancing the tiles in stalls

the shadow under the viaduct was them and became mine
Wrigley building clock five minutes too fast
shoes are squeaking, three men slowly cross the parking lot
five or six one street over
they seem not to be them
nor does the woman at the bottom of a staircase

it is the slow screech of the tracks
or on/off of ventilation that will take us
the blond stepping from the escalator
does not seem concerned
rather content as it rolls away from her
something is wrong by the Wilson station
they must have gripped those silver ridges on the roof
or swung on turns in between cars
it jerks—doors eventually open
light blue paper scratches the glistening floor

Ode to Yvette Vickers

I can't help but think of the blonde tufts on the bedroom floor
folding chair in a blue tube, taking up the entire room
all of those months and not enough mail to lure suspicion
I try to wonder who you are in the centerfold decades ago
putting jazz on the record player in only a white blouse
ashtray, bottle of wine with glasses, sandals, an open book of poems
right knee off the edge of a muted yellow couch
a grin that is everything July and a time between wars and romances
this is you before Reaganomics, a phone not in its cradle,
wary notes of passing cars between recipes in a notebook
computer screen glinting and the space heater hums while you shift from your heart

Proposing to Miss Make-Believe

I approached the point of boy wishing for girl. Hold hands in the big kids playground. Though every Alison or Lindsay had the word mystery for themselves, almost could there have been more.

A house in the neighborhood that I'd pass with my first bike. Never cars in driveway. The door with windows like prisms, so if there ever were to be a silhouette, it'd be hysterical, unclear.

There must have been a princess inside the house. Someone too pretty for afternoons. I no longer just passed. I began parking the blue bike with style. With a kickstand. Pretending a problem in the wheels or chain. I wanted the princess to see some kind of a true man, a mechanic. And while appearing to know what to fix, I'd peer through the spokes to see merely a hint of her. Yet nothing moved behind prism glass. The drapery didn't flinch. So for twin summers I rode home, disappointed.

Red Hands near Six Lanes

it wasn't the grey walls or to tower an unaccustomed staircase
eventually it would be the room slippery with blood
to pry for answers from whomever was left, panting
they turn out to be high school classmates from years ago
crowded like the wheelbarrows full of prisoners hanged at Buchenwald
sixty-five pairs of arms begging at the ankles

once again having evaded the past from a square building
stopping a cab and onto the highway, worried
every once in awhile another car
like the US-10 prior to first light as it approaches the hem of Detroit
in a glimpse the driver collapses with a gunshot
outside of the glass moaning becomes nearer

After the Funeral, Hamburg

I don't remember all of the forget-me-nots
birds far past morning and green in fields then streets
girls giggling full sentences like hiccups as bikes skim cobblestones
boys playing soccer from school to home for dinner
the walk ends with girls in dresses and glasses pretending a toll booth
asking us for driver's licenses or money to pass
"Freurshein zeigen oder twanzig pfennig bitte"
it breaks with more laughter and dancing in circles

ER, Friday Night

Jimmy Buffett on the radio as I drive there
not recalling the kitchen table moved for air
agree to check in at nine and try to relax
'Cheeseburger in Paradise' before automatic doors
the woman with an ankle brace and faltering words
inside a boy cries as if something is getting pulled out of his body
the couple on the other side of a curtain watch the news
he comments on every headline while I cough into my elbow
another man has a dog bite and I ponder the birthing room
son and daughter
the last time in one of these hallways someone was heaving
she pushed for what seemed like an hour
tonight the sounds and blood seem muted
except for the reporter and roommate
that boy and his mother taking care of him
three prescriptions, two x-rays,
one hour and forty-five minutes
Grateful Dead up Sacramento Avenue
'Friend of the Devil' is over by the Walgreens parking lot,
police in front of the door

At Mr. Weiner's

is this what we have without our ladies by the end?
soot around the refrigerator
black bags pyramided against the wall of a living room
sawdust in the basement
our grandson running up and down stairs
Friday until Sunday to be found in our woodshop

the globe is what draws me in
its mountain ranges raised
the fact that it was his
also in his classroom
gloves for gardening
Mrs. Doubtfire on VHS

his former wife takes me to the garage for the wooden
crafts in shopping bags and tupperware
again, along each wall
I am walking into the (dis)organized mind of his
she opens the door, turns on the light
I say, "I can't believe all of this"
"yeah," she replies, "try living with it"
"I can imagine," I say as she walks out of the door

well over an hour of sifting, rearranging, trying not to spill
the unused lumber on top of bags
all of these trinkets that made who he was in my classroom
bookends, cars, desk organizers, name plates, popsicle sticks
sandpaper, tubes, crayons, colored pencils,
unused plastic bags
just enough room to maneuver a car in
I can't believe he's gone
as is the woman who drives by in the alley, reversing
asking me if I'm his son
seeing him at her work down the street
not believing it with his energy and demeanor

On Seeing *I, Robot*, By Myself

yes, a near unblemished apocalypse,
compliments of the machines
Chicago, 2035 and I have to walk into downtown
after the fact
alone beginning with the longest credits I can recall
why must the moon be full tonight?
buildings all of a sudden hint too futuristic
and everywhere I look, those grey beings
too pale for aliens
back of my *X-Files* hat reads, "Fight the Future"
while discman declares, "defend the future"
"tonight we light the fires, we call our ships to port
tonight we walk on water, and tomorrow we'll be gone"
"oh great," I think, perfect timing
pacing underneath all the streets
which resemble something of horror from *The Terminator*
so I step onto a train
need I remind you of the moon?
fluorescent lights and wishing it will turn out okay
an ad says, "Remember what Mom said about sharing."
and somehow that won't matter one day
yes, a near unblemished apocalypse,
compliments of the machines

When Tucson Came for Amanda

you must have bathed five or six times to calm the ache in bones
that night at the Marriott on Michigan Avenue
without a pinch for the weekend
by noon curls still damp and you're sitting on the bed with a cigarette
drapes open, left breast braced by the white bathrobe
we walk for soup in one of the old restaurants
I tell you we're close over and over again

half the girls this Passover are reminiscent of you
yet curls have been cut, straightened, nearly bobbed

you talk of blood and glass next door
noises throughout the night
soon it's summer at Red Roof Inn
vacancy, welcome home

a child on the train tells Grandma he can count to 100
skipping from thirty-nine to ninety to his reflection in the tunnel

somewhere on Grand the sun sinks

Tribune Tower boasting the flag from its gothic tip
traffic loops into the pier
all those heads and I can't listen

your luck once came when the maid found you
legs stiff, thinned, hair sprawled on the carpet in morning
but there was a breath
and for months a cane, television, classic novels with a blue throw

I talk to Christa in the parking lot of a Monday night meeting

another chair is empty
sobbing I ask into the phone, "where are these people going?"
I am the last to leave

October begins with a five-year-old explaining the arrival of unicorns
she tells me, "I live in another future"

somehow your father has found me
says it's about you, is brief
I told you I told you I love you I told you I told you
never such messages of you like Meghan
so I walk back and forth with his throat
want to slip into that lake

let muck sift in the ears of Tucson and a noose
yet the refrain on concrete, together we choke

he asks for photographs and a eulogy
I had forgotten that your father calls you Mandy

the marching band keeps its distance
playing 'Centerfold' in strapped red hats

meanwhile the dreams begin
I find you near a dock on some boat
love yous, miss yous, and we're holding hands
over seven months will pass until we're sitting in a psych ward
you're pointing to things that aren't there
I'm telling you they aren't there
the young woman in the next bed hints at pretending to see the objects
I do
your eyes have become different, face longer, perspiration
our glances don't meet but I'm with you

the last time not in dreams was a limousine ride

diner, Walgreens, photograph with your eyes closed
onto Glenwood Avenue behind tinted windows back to Detroit in January

a couch, kleenex, snapshots of a family on vacation, even
your former piano teacher
gone two months to that city
I vowed to you of not being hurt

I stand at the podium with all those heads
now I can hear them, quiet
gaze at your parents and brother in the front row
previous to Streisand and you must be laughing at all of it

eighteen days from now I'll hang my black suit
if I could have held up your feet, gripped your thighs
then touched your neck for air
I would have cut that fucking rope
each twine with dust unsprung into one ignored and unforgettable moment
wait for a gasp
carry you from the porch into a desert morning

I park at your mother's after the funeral
one by one they land on the windshield
walking from the car, up the driveway, ladybugs cover my suit
others notice, try to brush them off
I know what you meant
I know that you've arrived safely

III.

Painting at First Light

everything prior to it has an unusual fitting
streets emptied a bit too early
the car accident with either blood or oil
a passenger's hat, an island within glass
then card games with friends until
Whitman's pigeons nearly as lovers at the Belmont station
once in this city have I seen them
flutter wings on rooftops like mad dancers
this morning the female flies away first
going south, the male waits until north

after all the obscene shards the brush is still there
despite quiet
this shall be mass without candles
thoughts set in line with the staining of hands
finally looking like man's skin
this isn't prayer but might as well be
with all these birds intuitive of spring
all this pause for brushes and rollers
a room for those intending renewal

The Southbound Untitled

I photographed Whitman once in this park
during another of these walks
there is the obvious of him
soil, birds, stumps, yet
the boys have strayed from the playground
swings are too much with rain

trees remain bowed in North Pond
their heads drowning into leaves
somehow branches have bloomed
from their skulls by early May

when I saw Whitman he was a reflection
a building in the bank of green water
little upside down hatchets of grass
funny how heroes can be perfectly placed
into rectangles

isn't it appropriate that the sky is birthing?
only few are paralyzed in cities of such
the old men with umbrellas
woman in a red raincoat
watches empty docks formed into a crucifix

some of us are watching Walt
it shall not be the last visitation

A Peninsula as Lover Then Son

somehow it was warm enough
unbuttoning each other's shirts, lips to neck
then sinking until your chest was to night
weeks until May

we unclasp as a car parks in front of the split rail wood fence
drape once the silhouette approaches
the officer politely cites a closed park
her flashlight on our quieted breathing and bench

it is not a strange place
as a boy Papa and I rode our bikes here
over a mile of dirt road until dusk and the lake
once there was a ten-speed bike, clothes clumped on the seat
unaware of a stranger past the curved end of dry sand
facing the same way as us, hands on surface like a sculptor
slowly into dark water upon her waist
we peered into shoulders and arms
all else below lily pads seemed without motion
then Papa and I turned
feet to pedals for home with dust to a lake never the same

To Downtown in July

I pass the lovers who dare
allow waves to wrap the waist
without lifeguards well into night
tide becomes spittle against concrete
what is found doesn't match
like water to no sand
the solitary to tourist couples
moon above neon of the Drake Hotel

Starved in the Accidental

"In rivers the water you touch is the last of what has passed and the first of that which comes; so with time present."
—Leonardo Da Vinci, 1200 Alberni Street, Vancouver, B.C., Canada

again finding myself at a lodge
and I haven't shaved since Seattle
prepared
       under trees
              for this

yet superstitions have refused to work
in the week

the waitress talks of rain like a body
having memorized arrival
figure, motives, the stay
rivers lie dry for us to imagine their flooding

once more without your hands in the tilting
canyons, water against it, we know of that
leaving our initials etched to find return
even ladybugs are different here

a bat circling where it echoes
just like when I was a boy
a glimpse of it with leaves while floating
where all I wanted was that home and the sounds
of nothing, the woods, a far off motorcycle
even the train from miles
and so reintroductions ensue
herons wait on the dam
travelers I hear—may we purchase the hour of goodnight
and wish off the river like they must have done

Six Bags of Barbie

on arrival the beds are covered
headboards with unopened dinette sets
something to do with a wedding
all NRFB they say—Not Removed From Box

nine floors of the Hyatt and countless accessories
pink heels, silver pots, green knit sweaters and the hangers
then stories—husbands with their doll-obsessed wives
having traveled from Oregon, or it's their seventh convention
the collectors continue with
"she's very pretty"
"that's the original box"
"it's quite a collection really"

David and I carry the pink bags
all the while asking for Mulder and Scully Barbie
which no one has
then I come to learn of the recall edition
where Scully's hair was too long
and so the more appropriate above the shoulders trim was released
but is worth a bit less, of course

I've never seen so much nakedness
long legs and eyelashes bunched in tupperware
heads for five dollars each, sometimes six or seven
I flip through the box till the perfect memento
the blonde head of P.J.
and David tells me it's a nice one

Descent into Denver

this must be the place
pines dotted in a prologue to rivulets
pools like concrete first mixing with water
a velvet trail from middle of the highway
has thinned into the wind of farms

Geronimo, I can't find you on the ridge
horses run riderless into honeyed grasses
where are the baseball diamonds? little towns?
the cliffs, suburbs, empty
maybe the propellers or landing gear causing to hide
the silhouettes I expected since leaving Sedona at six
I imagine it's freedom that pushes them halfway to dusk

To Downtown in October

I begin swayed into a night crawl
awakening at dark, then coffee and TV dinner
from the bus—statues, trees in parks, and former cemeteries
silence until a skyline
shall evening be as gentle as it once was?

White Mist at Bunker Hill

in between the trees each field has no more
than two feet of it
stillness below a constant sky
Sunday night arrivals and no moon
just above the cloud-like grass is solely the outline of
branches
further up, constellations in a slight blur

silhouettes have disappeared from each pavilion
flickering lighters and lulled conversations
autumn for one week
the path without couples or bikes
the getaway before work resumes

prior to noises being unrecognizable in the oaks
cicadas or squirrels well after sunset
the rip of an acorn through leaves
a skunk shuffling in the front yard, tail raised
stains in the parking lot

Vater, Ich Schlafe Nicht or Father, I Am Not Sleeping

I am beginning to somewhat sleep like my father
one arm underneath the other
pale side posed to ceiling
outstretched far past the bed's end
though he faces the window, wall
and I the rest of this room

always have I been among the wild sleepers
the top sheet spiraling into a frenzied rope
until the routine unraveling
bottom sheet losing at least one corner
posture does change
even in sleeping as it has

but tonight I have hours until rest
days and years until something less calm than this
the impossible city sky reveals its last
middle-night summer stars
this rooftop and sixty-one small secrets with oneself
spread before me like an old sauntering battle
with no one else watching
no one to give it permission
to depart

Dusk and the Daughter Named Isabel

water flat as never is
fireworks days and days early
this week we're neighbors at the beach
your mother calls you in running with others near rocks
you are bye-byeing the sun
never hesitate at the deep of lake

10:07 p.m.   each detail of cloud, scratches, lightness
                       in how late it has suddenly become

not once to decide whether blue past trees
remind of Renoir or Monet

10:09 p.m.   two deer at the side of road, the abandoned
                       house passed unseen
                       hay bales not yet in fields

it has been too long since this
or the sands of Charlevoix, Grand Haven, Manistee

10:13 p.m.   the half moon, schoolhouse
                       with its rusted bell and ancient teeter-totters

the man stuttering of sailboats
a scent of herring from my hands

10:19 p.m.   the third deer for tonight
                       fog over street after rain is still there

washing hands, wrists, mouth
before dinner and another night of quietness
little one, I wish you many unique gifts
may you never leave these dunes

IV.

Dealey Plaza

even at ten months my son isn't too new for history
in a stroller on the sixth floor peering into family photos and
whitewall tires
as usual, patient and content with all of us in close rooms
suddenly there is glass squared by the window
awry stacks of boxes stamped, 'Scott Foresman and
Company'
the curve in pavement from Houston Street, slope, over-
pass, my boy
I suppose for my parents and in-laws November faintly is
September to us
by the opposite corner of the floor my son's grandpa begins
to question distance and Oswald alone at chess

outside, in part, a few of us become fractured
a white X on Elm Street for the last shot
lawn too flourished for July in Texas
where the man with a black umbrella stood, waiting
my son and I pose for the camera with the plastic wheel that
winds film
in front of the book depository and on grass
close to Bill and Gayle Newman, having lain over their small
children
by 7:30 the cicadas have quieted
where have they disappeared to so quickly?

On Seeing *The Revenant*, By Myself

outside theater #3 a cab driver waits with the moon
while Hugh keeps warm in a horse carcass
remembering his son
I don't notice the white sky until the parking lot
ignition in three degrees Fahrenheit
drive toward it for the best photo
slanted, bottom half is shown
behind the grocery store for a clearing
inch slowly until rid of trees and signs
the window downed, zoom in
lacking pixels but try to take what I remember about it
I grab my boy at home, 1:11 a.m.
my turn for him to dream next to me
"I am here, I am here"
carry him downstairs and speak of how much he is cared for
he sputters, "I love you," with eyes still closed
on the orange futon I cover his shoulders with a blanket

To Bryce or Victoria

tonight a full moon I wonder who you will be
boy or girl, your smile, in which way exuberant
how you will stroll into love
like your brother be passionate about cars
or dinosaurs for you, paintings, or skyscrapers?

tonight there are still ugly things
a young lady rips her hand from the gentleman
who leans over and says something
rust on white columns below train tracks
a woman on the movie screen sobs to her knees
dripping from her nose in front of a 1950s furnace
cold fast food cheeseburgers when suddenly it's the next
day
and potholes too many to estimate

tonight in six weeks at last you arrive
we in a place only for you
your breathing, giggling, crying, yawning
the dreamed of, desired soul to sway in great-grandmother's
rocking chair
to rid the flaws of being a Friday night passerby

April in Harbor Springs

hawks having arrived in semi-circles above shadows from the birches
having lengthened over the interstate's four lanes
a crow picks at the beginning of grass from pavement

years since this drive and now Victoria's alphabet from the backseat
the car in front of the three of us
Blake asks Oma and Opa, "are we there yet?" every five minutes

once there, the tide has fallen, adding a peninsula of rocks
gulls louder as I step closer for a photo from the fog
several duck skeletons from their feet not taking from mulchy sand
bill, ribs, legs in granules and seaweed by the stones in a circle
five 'sand cakes' made by Blake and Oma
insistent wind and two toy trucks parked

A Day with My Daughter

waking up jovial despite the rain
books from the crib to downstairs
the two of us, you without your brother
your mother knows these mornings better
five scrambled eggs with your fingers
pieces on your lap then floor
watching the garbage truck, waving and asking about its
sounds
"I'm a princess" over and over
reading 'The Witch Lady,' by Nancy Carlson, to me
Dora and a haunted gingerbread house—jellybeans, bats,
bones
Tommy Dorsey on the radio to the grocery store
overcast while looking at pumpkins

Summer Drive

hints of haziness and sixty-six degrees
Billy Idol's 'Hot in the City' plays between songs from *Frozen*
sung by my kids after the video store
Shermer Road in the late afternoon, a few skunks to side

keep pondering those rooms at 3930 North Pine Grove
at six, Michael losing his father
sought after conclusions before turning fifty
prayer with the woman at Cook County Morgue

everyone is elated
another red light in a cool, cloudless suburb
a young lady sings with the window down
back seat, henna on her right hand, about to turn left

Home in Nine Moons
~for Blake & Victoria

we're driving to the moon tonight
on just over 1/4 tank and Britney Spears on KISS FM
there it hangs, smoldered orange above the streetlights
seven flights underway to O'Hare
we'll strike matches, throw them, see if the orange is flammable

your hands still move on a knitted blanket
looking into the forest preserve on a right turn
Neil Young sings of deserts as the rain begins
this afternoon Grandma cried because you did
I assured her you're exhausted

six dollar fish 'n chips special tonight
the teachers say you have a calm spirit
your head sideways on a blanket after the hearing
another school being closed
I can't tell if you're enamored with the architecture of faces
at Monroe and LaSalle
we weave through Friday night I-94 lanes
like Al Pacino until the Cadillac in *Heat*
yet we rush for jamies, milk, Nina and her puppet friend, Star

one wouldn't think it looked like the end of the world
too light and yellow for 8:45 at night
here we are, nine cars waiting at the drive-thru
you lean forward to watch the lightning north of the Wendy's parking lot
frosty cup twirling in an empty space
orange flowers rocking under pigtails
rearview mirror flashes, pedestrians unconcerned
Peter Gabriel's 'Shock the Monkey' as we wait for a #3, large, with two double stacks
a woman on a bike, plastic bag wavering with groceries on the right handle

like clockwork you ask for a fry

we walk out of Subway and you're still holding onto the ATM receipt
you point it out in English and German
the pre-valentine harvest moon above the strip mall
in the car, turning the corner of the movie theater parking garage you find it once more
the singer on the radio talks of howling at it
so it goes "na na" behind the trees
your mother calls it "beautiful, gorgeous" above Devon Avenue

most of the leaves on concrete
with Alicia Keys singing about morning love
dogs, bikers in shorts
Indian summer begins one week before Halloween
Amtrak #177 passes as Toni Braxton sings down the sun behind a warehouse
Victoria cries at another red light
2/3 moon

Victoria's asleep
Little Caesars in the front seat
Enigma's 'Return to Innocence' on the 90s countdown on 101.1 FM
I tell Blake it is one of my favorite songs
he shows me his matchbox car (a white, Nissan Skyline GTR R34)
onto Northwest Highway on a Friday night
these are the streets of your mother's first years
Blake points out the barber, Trader Joe's
Elm Street is getting dark
the Pickwick Theatre, P-I-C of the restaurant flickering

Bob Dylan sings about 'pretty people'
storm quickly whips branches
pothole is nearly filled
the moon is on the other side of grey

last night it was behind clouds, dangerous
Blake asks to roll up my window since rain is coming in
this week you're concerned over thunder
Victoria has taken her shoes off
the lights on Touhy are off near the bookstore

the radio traffic announces twenty-two minutes downtown
on the interstate from north to south
Blake's mouth is wide open
facing away from the smudged crescent moon
clouds low on the horizon
Victoria's saying "mommy" between words like a character
from *Star Wars*
no trains tonight while Ellie Goulding sings of outer space
and a fire
I can't stop thinking about the Newmans
so close to see the president
then a face like pink cabbage
crouching over their children
it will be fifty years in two weeks

Black Friday

the three of us walk into cold without wind
down streets after chiefs and tribes
pass the playground by the tracks, four new slides
only the sandbox has stayed the same
Victoria asks to play while Blake waves twigs as swords
then post office and gift cards for their mother
nails being painted while a movie blares on a flat screen
the hair salon is close so we continue by another park
we talk about watching *A League of Their Own* there in June
I tell them about my Sunday afternoon walks with their
grandparents when I was little
hours with the crunch of snow, whooshing of pants
through the woods behind Aretha Franklin's house
just the three of us, like today
those long, black shadows of the trees
each blizzard with sun I think of those walks
Victoria "lalala's" down Sauganash Avenue
content with her stuffed dog in the stroller

Joris Soeding's most recent chapbooks are Yellow Shift and Unruly (*Night Garden Journal*, 2018) and In Between the Places Where Night Falls (*Lummox Press*, 2015). Soeding's writing has appeared in publications such as *Another Chicago Magazine, Belle Rêve Literary Journal, The Ladies and Gentlemen of Horror Anthology,* and *Red River Review.* He is a 7th/8th grade Social Studies teacher in Chicago, where he resides with his wife, son, and daughter.